What Seas?
What Shores?

What Seas?
What Shores?

H S Shivaprakash

BLACK EAGLE BOOKS
2020

BLACK EAGLE BOOKS

USA address:
7464 Wisdom Lane
Dublin, OH 43016

India address:
E/312, Trident Galaxy, Kalinga Nagar,
Bhubaneswar-751003, Odisha, India

E-mail: info@blackeaglebooks.org
Website: www.blackeaglebooks.org

First International Edition Published by
BLACK EAGLE BOOKS, 2020

WHAT SEAS? WHAT SHORES?
by H S Shivaprakash

Original Copyright © **H S Shivaprakash**

All rights reserved. No part of this publication may be reproduced, stored in a retrieval system, or transmitted, in any form or by any means, electronic, mechanical, photocopying, recording or otherwise without the prior permission of the publisher.

Cover & Interior Design: Ezy's Publication

ISBN- 978-1-64560-104-3 (Paperback)
Library of Congress Control Number: 2020943431

Printed in United States of America

PREFACE

This volume includes my poems written from 2015 onwards. The occasions of the composition are widely different. So were the places, people and situations that inspired them. Because this period for me was one of hectic travels through different countries and continents. I do not remember very clearly whether they were written in English or in my own language Kannada. I hold myself responsible both to the language I was born into and the language I had to acquire for my professional needs. For more than three decades, I was monogamously wedded to writing in my own language. But as a result of my temporary residences in places where my language was not spoken or understood, I had to resort to English, which was neither my language nor theirs, but a convenient link language between us. For me, poetry is a means of communication with people and places. This is how my writing became bilingual. Working between two widely different languages, Kannada, a member of the Dravidian language family and English, a language of the Germanic branch of Indo-Aryan languages, has made me more sensitive to the possibilities and limitations of both these mediums of poetry.

Like most poetry in the contemporary world, I see my poetry as a desperate search for one's own root in a world condemned to rootlessness; rootlessness not just because people and communities are uprooted but also because cultural and psychological displacements and dislocations even in the same geographical spaces, we once saw as unified. So now the home is everywhere and nowhere. All of us who have eyes to see and hearts to feel are now acutely aware of the paradox of continuities among disjunctions. These poems inhabit the same precarious space-time and attempt to live out its dialectics.

I am deeply grateful to all my friends from my own language area and the rest of the world who liked and admired these poems. I am also grateful to my fellow poet-translators who rendered some of these poems into other languages: Zingonia Zingone, Carlos Agaso, Clara Agnes, Ricardo Rubio, Johanna Carvajal who translated them into Spanish; Khalid Risouni who translated them into Arabic. A handful of these poems were also translated into Portuguese, Romanian, and Lithuanian by different translators. My heartfelt thanks are due to all of them. I am thankful to my dear friend Prof. Sumanyu Satpathy for agreeing to write a warm introduction to this book and to the Mexican poet Marlene Pasini for writing the blurb.

I express my deep gratitude to Mr. Satya Patnaik for coming forward to publish this volume. I now invite my readers to accompany me in this journey through many restless days and sleepless nights in far-flung places and times, real and imagined.

HS SHIVAPRAKASH
New Delhi 31-07-2020

THE POET AS A SNAKE CHARMER

In the crowded marketplace of contemporary poetry, it is difficult to sift grain from chaff. As a result, one ends up chaffing about the glut of poetry in every Indian language, and certainly in English;and its reception limited to the poet's own circle of friends and family members. A decade ago, poets in India complained about publishers not being able to publish much poetry as there were hardly any patrons of poetry, the shrinking reading public preferring prose fiction to poetry. With the increasing popularity of blog and social media, poets seem to be having a good time. The other day, a leading Odia poet complained to his facebook users that these days, poetry appreciation is reduced to smileys, red hearts and likes. Surely, readers, he said, could type a few words if only to indicate that they had read his poems! Fortunately for HS Shiva Prakash, Kannada poet and playwright, there has been no dearth of audience in his mother tongue since he began publishing.

It is quite possible that his father, a Lingayat scholar himself, and with a Shiva in his own name, named him after the presiding deity. Having listened to his inner drumbeatfairly early, Shiva Prakashsoon realised his calling as a poet, and published his first collection of poetry, Milarepa (1977) when he was still a student. It was noticed by poetry lovers and discerning critics as the work of a distinctive voice. His popularity grew further with the publication of his second volume in 1983. In fact, since then, he has been a popular poet and dramatist whose work is always awaited in eager anticipation. However, it was still limited only to the Kannada audience. Around the turn of the century, his works began to be translated into English and other Indian languages. I think the turning point came with his appointment as Director, Tagore Centre, Berlin. Of late, both the poet and his poetry have taken to frequent travelling, as Shiva keeps gettinginvited all over the world, enjoying a global audience. His poetry readings are nothing short of a sensation, for the reason that his metres, diction and rhythm are organically tied to his thoughts; it is almost as if he still belongs to the oral tradition. In fact, my first entry into Shiva's poetical world in Kannada—which was a long time ago—was through his readings, though I did not at once understand them. Of course, he offered impromptu translations into English, and that is when I understood his popularity and greatness. His work stood out from among a galaxy of well-known poets—at least a dozen—who too followed the same strategy, but the magic of sound and sense was missing in their readings.

It is wonderful that Shiva has started composing his new poetry in English, and the collection here is one among his recent creations. Before commenting on the poems here, I wish to say a few words about what I find so attractive and exclusive about his poetry. For one thing, though one does not wish to run down Indian poetry in English per se,

I tend to be somewhat partial about those bilingual poets who have lived and are familiar with their own poetical tradition, straddling two or more traditions. If they had written only in their own language and a non-poet, say, and academic, and, not the poet himself/herself, had translated the poetry into English, I would not be too excited. But, if it is translated into one of the Indian languages I know, I would savour it more. In any case, when such a bilingual poet writes in English, and I am speaking of the best such as Arun Kolatkar and AK Ramanujan, and a host of poets from India's north-eastern languages, the poetry comes across as very strong, breathing the local tradition and soil. Here, I am especially fond of, apart fromKolatkar's poetry, the work of Desmond Kharmawphalang and Robin S Ngangom. Apropos, I had once interviewed Louise Bernice Halfe, a Cree poet and social workerinSaskatoon, Canada,. Her Cree name itself sounded so fascinating, to me, at least, when translated to English (Sky Dancer), I asked her about the special tone and idiom in her poetry. She confessed to me that, though she wrote originally in English, she conceived every word, every single idea in her "native" tongue, and translated these into English. If not as radically—since upper caste Indian bilingual poets, even the Khasis, Meitis and Aos, seem to have internalised the English ethos and idiom—one does find a special flavour in the best of such poetry. It is as if they keep translating their thoughts and ideas in their own language and translating (carrying across) these into English. Whenever I have pointed this issue of language out to Shiva, he says two things. One, that many of his recent poems may have been composed in Kannada and translated into English, or vice versa. This reminds me of a few poems of Kolatkar which he had composed in English and translated into

Marathi; but which appeared in a collection of Marathi poems. Desmonds poems, similarly, appeared in a collection edited by Nigel Jenkins in Wales, with a note saying that they were translations from Khasi. Far from being unethical, these are facts that the poets understand. The second point is that his poetry draws on medieval Tamil / ancient Sangam poetry as his mother came from that background. It is this special flavour in Shiva Prakash's poetry that has drawn me to it. I have been familiar with his poetry for close to two decades. I especially enjoy listening to him in a quiet corner during sessions of carousal.

The indigenous tradition I am referring to here and to which Shiva belongs is the Shaivite Bhakti tradition, whereas the Vaishnava form of Bhakti is dominant, thanks to what I call the "Chaitanya cosmopolis". Shiva's poetry is almost oxymoronically crossbred, inspired as it is by Lingayat mysticismand Marxism. It is also influenced by Lal Ded's Shaivism. There has always been a strain of the incantatory in his poetry. Just as Tagore's mature poetry reminds us of Kabir and the Baul songs, so do Shiva's Kannada poems of the Kannadvachan poetry. They are sometimes epigrammatic and allusive. True to the tradition, many of the poems by Shiva Prakash begin and end with an invocation of a mystic Shiva.

O Guru Shivalinga
The two zeros are the two signs
You have given
Thank you! (The Two Zeros)

This reminds me of what Tejaswini Niranjana says about the linga, which "is/is not Shiva or God; it is a form for formlessness, a shape for shapelessness". In fact, such a paradoxical attitude is typical of the medieval liminal language. This explains how Shiva can be both a believer and a Marxist.

The opening poem, "Tonight" sets the tone. The murder and the rapist can sleep peacefully, he says. But Shiva the poet cannot.

> But this unfortunate creature
> The poet Shivaprakash
> Cannot sleep
> For he is condemned
> To weep not only for the murdered
> And the raped
> But also with perpetrators
> Who murder and rape themselves.

This Shaivite is not otherworldly as he is enraged by the crime being perpetrated by heartless fellow humans. The poet is "bitten by the horrible snake".

> Beloved is his lord Neelakantha
> The Blue-throated one".

The "horrible" snake can mean one or all of the mythological symbolism associated with it and as Shiva's ornament. It is supposed to be an embodiment of ahamkara, which Shiva has defanged. With humans, the ego remains untamed and is dangerous or "horrible". The Vachana poets too traditionally comment on the evil that humans perpetrate. The following lines carrying the metaphor of mustard are drawn on AllamaPrabhu:

> Whenmustard turns into an ocean
> In the cells of bones and muscles
> Mustards to mustards
> O Shiva O Hara
> Pain painpain
> Vaster than the ocean

> Deeper than the ocean
> No joy in the ocean
> Not even in the mustard
> Was it, is it there
> In you?
> [The Moment's Hunt]

But, of course, the mustard symbolism is rather secular as it is used by the scriptures and teachings in Buddhism, Judaism, Christianity and Islam. Truly enough, the Buddha surfaces in Shiva's poem on Ambedkar, drawing attention to social injustice. As I have already said, these poems are as much about all the wrong and painful happenings in the world as they are about ways of achieving inner peace. They disturb and alarm us, put the "horrible snake" around our neck, they also tell us how to get rid of it. They jolt our ego; yet they offer our soul solace. The mysticism in Shiva's poetry is not escapist, not an escape from the real, everyday world. Nor is their worldliness an invitation to cynicism. They offer us what powerful poetry unfailingly does. Shiva! Shiva!

- Sumanyu Satpathy

CONTENTS

Tonight	17
William Tell and the Apple: A Parable Retold	18
Your Shore	20
Babasaheb's Land of Initiation	22
Says Odysseus	24
Earth and Water	25
What Should We Do With Rapists	26
Do Not Go	28
I Don't Want To Say Goodbye	30
A Greek Love Poem	32
Buddha to Angulimala	33
Goodbye, city	35
Sleep My Heart Sleep	36
Dark Goddess	37
Waiting	39
Spring in Santiago	40
Tonight This Body	42
Survival	45
The White Moon	46
Another Dreamship	47
Jesus On The Hill, Rio De Jenero	49
Stubborn Heart	51
Just a Little Longer	53
Anywhere	55
Last Supper	57
We Too Shall Pass	59
The World Theatre Day Poem	61
When Touch Is Tabooed	63
The Two Wings	66
Says an Aboriginal Girl	67
Rain in San Jose	68

Severed Head	69
Two Zeroes	70
Winter is My Season	72
The Conqueror	74
Seeking You	76
Silence	77
My Beloved City	79
Kolkata	81
Why Not Leave Ageing Cities Alone	82
When the Poet Went to Sleep	84
One Moment	86
Take off Your Shoes	88
The Tavern	90
When Thousands are Dying	92
I Told You	94
The Moment's Hunt	96
The Black Flower	97
Three Mothers	98
Last Night	100
Pain	102
Tiresias Warns	104
Medea Matters	105
What City? What Light?	107
Do Not Wait Rajdip	108
The Poet's Silence	110
AnAnti-Poem	111
To Monsinor Romero	113
A Sudden Glance	114
The Desert	115
Tiny Blue Flower	116
Exile	117
Your Name	118
The Lotus	120
Like A Pearl	122
Crocodile	123
Do Not Thank	124
The Priest	125
On Your Face	126
Farewell	127
Two Green Spirits	128
Tangiers, Morocco	129
While in Chalkidiki, Greece	131
The Rainbow	132
Why Write Poetry?	133
Playthings	134

Tonight

Tonight
Is the night
When even
The murderer and the murdered
The rapist and the victim
Can sleep peacefully
The murderer and the rapist
Have had their way
The murdered and the rape victims
Are either dead or half dead
But this unfortunate creature
The poet Shivaprakash
Cannot sleep
For he is condemned
To weep not only for the murdered
And the raped
But also with perpetrators
Who murder and rape themselves
For he is bitten by the horrible snake
Beloved is his lord Neelakantha
The Blue-throated one.

William Tell and the Apple: A Parable Retold

Said the master to the slave William Tell:

'It is the scum and dregs of the earth
like you
Who have eaten up all the apples
of the earth
so that noble people like us are denied

Now just one apple is left in the world-
that one
balanced delicately
on the head of your one and only son

There are two arrows:
one in my hand and another in yours

Let us have a fair match
If your arrow strikes the apple first
it's yours
if mine strikes it first, it's mine

Remember:
if either of us misses the mark
the victim is not the apple
but your poor son

So
if you want your son,
the apple is mine
Otherwise
It's for you to decide

Your Shore

If I reach your shore
Some day
I will bring you a fistful of my earth
A few blades of grass
A drop of water from our river
And the ray of our sun
That led me to you
Through wind and water

If I reach your shore
Some night
I will bring my companion star
That lit up my sleep and dreams
And that crescent part of the moon
Which I rowed and rode
On the earth and on the sky
Looking for you
And your shore

If I come
By day or night
In a dream or wakefulness
I will bring our dethroned gods
And their goddesses
Waiting to reincarnate

On your shore
In human forms

Even if I forget
My earth et cetera
I will surely bring this
Incomplete poem
For you to complete

I am the father
And you, the daughter
I am the voyage
And you, the shore

Babasaheb's Land of Initiation

This is the land of initiation
The land where birth goes through a death
The place of being reborn
After dying
Not in the idle talk of those
Good- for-nothings, nincompoops
Blind by birth
Who speak of birth after birth after birth
But existing in open-eyed expanse of
Wakefulness of Buddha's awareness
In the auspicious vision of truth
Where those condemned and cornered
In untouchability are freed
On the unshakable foundation
Of freedom by rebirth in this very birth

This is the Diksha bhoomi
Of Ambedkar's truth
Which was the place of new birth
For those trampled down
Into the abysm of untouchability

On this birthday of his
When a universal disease
Of 'don't touch' is spreading

This is the Diksha bhoomi for all
Both for the touchable and the untouchable
The land of Initiation of Buddha
The guru of gurus
And panacea of panaceas
In the season of painful penance

Says Odysseus

None of my fortune-tellers
Or divination experts know
That when I return to my kingdom
Victorious but ruined
Changed beyond recognition
Through age and countless ordeals

No-one will recognize me
My wife will have become tired
Of waiting
My son Telemachus
Will not recognize me
Neither will my subjects
Though I try to persuade them
That I am that legend Odysseus
Who razed the invincible Troy
No, none of them will believe
Except the maid who nursed me
When I was small
In spite of her growing senility

Yes, only I know
That this is how it will turn out
If at all my beloved Ithaca
Still stands
When I return

But may be it will not

Earth and Water

When earth and water united
The witness was a cloud
Which declared:
The water and the earth are together
For ever

The cloud moved on

When water and the earth separated
The witness was another cloud
Which declared:
The water and earth
Are fated
To be separated

The cloud moved on

But the earth and water
Can never be together
Neither can they part

What Should We Do With Rapists

What should we do
with rapists and murderers
who plead for mercy?

If you forgive them
they will not forgive you or the world
for forgiving them
but will go once again
on their raping and murderous spree

If you hang them with rope
shoot them with bullets
stone them to death
set them on fire
poison them with hemlock
they will be reborn
thousands more in number
like Raktabijasuras
fighting with Ma Durga

What should we do with them?
Whatever you do they come back

because they have their seeds
in depths of human heart
the venomous seeds
alongside seeds of immortality

Yes they will come back
in unexpected forms
till the fire of Shiva's third eye burns them
into ashes
till the oceans of Buddha's compassion
wash away those heaps of ashes

Do Not Go

Do not go my beloved
To the far-off land
Don't you see here
Autumn's magic wand?

Koels are singing aloud
Peacocks are cackling
Amidst desert sands
Gardens are booming

Into the vacant valley
Darkness is descending
From the clouds above
Torrents are cascading

On river bank
When I was waiting
Something would happen
I had an eerie feeling

O dear one, please
Stay close to me
Lest saffron flowers
Wither in the tree

A variety of fruits
Mixed with jaggery
Juices and their flavours
Bring us glee

Like into the blazing fire
Pouring ghee
That's how we are
You and me

Do not go O dear one
To the far-off land
Autumn is here
With his magic wand

(A Rajasthani folk song)

I Don't Want To Say Goodbye

I don't want say goodbye to you
If you go away
Who will maintain the garden
You planted
The sweetest dreams
That the earth ever dreamed
When tyrants have released
New insects
That threaten to eat up all plants

You planted the garden
But withheld from us
Undeserving ones
The gardener's secrets:
What healing music
And which precious mantras
Will guard the plants
From killer insects
And the tyrant who fathered them
In his hellish nightmares

The plants have now grown into trees
Which have burgeoned of late
About to flower
And then yield the promised fruits

That will satiate all hunger
Till the tyrant too
Will no more be so hungry
As to eat up our children

We will not say goodbye
Do not go

A Greek Love Poem

Descend into me
Like the blue sky
Into the bluer Cretan sea

Burst green from inside me
Like olive groves
From barren rocky hills

Purify my breath
Like the scent of thyme
Cleaning the air
Once again

Said Heraclitus:
'Never again
No man walks into the same river
Again'

I disagree:
'All of us do
Into the same river
For the sun sucks up the water
And returns it to the same
Through rain
Again
And again'
(Crete, 7.2.2018)

Buddha to Angulimala

How many more severed fingers
do you want to go into your stinking necklace
O Angulimala?
What monstrous passion
began to rage in your dark heart
to choose,
instead of flowers, pearls or diamonds,
severed human fingers
which were meant to grow crops
play music, write poems of love,
touch and heal an ailing body
to offer worship to gods
to paint, to sculpt, to shape
beautiful images...

No-one has a soul,
say Noble Ones
But who can think of humans
without hands

When you cut fingers
you kill humans
when you kill a human
you kill another potential Buddha
another chance to end sufferings
another chance of nirvana

You pull the world
which is also you
deeper into darkness and ignorance
to perpetuate the rule of Mara
the architect of suffering
for the living and non-living

Wake up from this nightmare
of Mara
into the light of freedom
and compassion

Throw away that stinking necklace
Cast away the ancient darkness
from your heart

Goodbye, city

Goodbye city
Reflected in me all night!
When your buildings stood
Lights shone
Two and four wheelers
Moved to and fro
I made them all still and moving
Move and tremble
Reflected and refracted
Moving and trembling
Like water
In my restless mirror-body
Goodbye
The dawn is around
I will no more reflect
Anything human and mortal
But the sky
Blue draped in light
Or covered with clouds
Till night comes round again

Sleep My Heart Sleep

Sleep my heart sleep
But my heart never sleeps
My voice is dying down
My arms are giving way
My heart does not listen
To my own heart singing
Sleep my heart sleep
Half the heart sings
Half the heart screams
Arson, loot, massacres
Drench the earth with blood
Screams and shouts
Rip the wind apart
Sleep my heart sleep
Bombs and grenades go off
Silence my heart silence
Explosions everywhere
Half my heart is the stubborn mother
Singing the lullaby non stop
Half my heart is the rebel son
Deaf and dead to her song
O when will the two hearts unite?
Will the father ever be the baby again
Breathing softly like a baby
And not like an unstoppable hurricane?

Dark Goddess

The sun and the moon
My companions
Since I came on this earth
The stars above that witness
My insomniac longing for you
You O Dark Goddess
The lamps that light up
temples and courtyard
Candles in the Church
Praying till they melt
Countless electric lamps and lights
That illuminate the long roads at night
The lonely street lamps dreaming silently
The torches that guide us
In remote villages with no power supply
The swarm of glowworms lighting up
Himalayan valleys in the dead of a new moon night
None of them can light you up
None of them can even see you
For the dark door of your palace
Of broken loving hearts
Of defeated howling spirits
With whom you reside
There is no key of light
I am sending cries

Into that womb of dark dark darkness
Invisible impenetrable darkness
O goddess
Bless me with eyes
That can find and see you
In the womb of primal darkness
In the cave of irremediable blindness
Where you
Wisdom beyond wisdom
Dwell and reign supreme

Waiting

A thunder
A soft breeze
A beam of light from the sun or moon
Just a tremor of an earth quake
Or a sudden spasm of pain
In the heart
A snake or an insect bite
The roar of a lion
The whining of a dog
Torrential rain in a famine struck land
One of these would bring
A brief message from you
A small token of acknowledgement
Of my waiting for you
For a whole life time
For many life times
For glimpse your sapphire splendor
O dark goddess
O my cradle and grave
O ecstasy of cremation grounds

No massage has come for centuries
In my time world
But just the flash of eyelids in yours

I go on waiting
Till death
Beyond death
For my waiting for your message
Will outlive my million deaths

Spring in Santiago

In the midst of brown leaves
On twigs and branches
The green leaves are shooting up
Slowly, surely and silently
Spring is coming to Santiago
On the heels of frozen winters

Suspended in time between
Winter and spring
The days are turning warm
While the nights
Touch you with cold fingers

Spring has returned
To the wintry city
Melting down hearts and waters
Like Krishna returning
To Brindavan
Jesus to Jerusalem
Bulbul to the rose garden
Greatest prosperity
To the poor of the world
And hope
To our exhausted earth

Every dawn and dusk
Every living thing
Has begun
to celebrate
Welcome back
O spring

Every living thing
Except me
Though you my spring have
Come and every living thing has
Begun to sing and celebrate:
'Welcome back spring!'
But not I for
My winter cannot recede
Making my spring song
To Santiago
An elegy to all my springs

Santiago de Chile
3.10.2019

Tonight This Body

Tonight
This body
A black river prone but not asleep
An ocean of the dark night...
The ship of my heart
Now floating now sinking
Is searching for
Past holocausts
All-swallowing deluges
That swallowed up
Ancient cities of splendour
Magnificent monuments of wonder
The most recent miracles
Eight, not eight but eighteen,
Not even that but eighteen
Thousand thousand
Man-made wonders
The incomparable glories
Of sea shore cities
Prisons bursting with
Brilliant instruments of brutal torture
The rope bridges across deepest valleys
The kailasas built on hilltops
The graveyards vast as the earth
The cradles even vaster

And beds as big as mind can imagine
Where sleep great emperors
And the poorest beggars
Next to each other
As if they are brothers
To each other
Dreaming the greatest treasures
Of the earth
And lethal weapons
Feigning the innocence of children
Where have they all gone
Tell me O Allamaprabhu
On the dark river
The ocean of the night
That keeps on asking this
Appears the reflection
Of a sky there
Or a shining galaxy
I remember with tears
Terrible, wasteful wars of the past
Friends and foes who died
Lovers who loved and lied
Despite their commitment
To truth
In equal numbers
In periods of war and peace
Of past, present and future
And the cities of the sun and moon
We intended to reach
But could not

Wake up Shivaprakash from
The oceans of sleep

Seven thousand leagues deep
Wake up with fish, crocodiles and whales
In the mists of the living dead
Of those who died but could not
Of yogis, pleasure-seekers, the sick
Who were celebrating
Each in his own way
The beginningless and the endless
In the evanescent

Wake up
Invoke
The great Rudras
With the mudras of boon and protection
Creating, nursing, destroying
Disappearing and compassion-giving
Praying for happiness here, hereafter
And a beautiful day
In this dark river
In this ocean of night
In this graveyard of great light

Survival

a whole people were liquidated
but I kept quiet
all rivers were poisoned
but I kept quiet
all lovers were parted
but I kept quiet

all words lost meanings
but I kept quiet
all memories were erased
at the click of the mouse
all love songs turned into hate and curses
but I kept quiet

I do not even seek your forgiveness
you cannot forgive somebody
who just wanted to save his skin
who just became a survivor
and forgot completely
how to live
like herbs and flower

The White Moon

The White moon
That shone bright the other evening
In my garden full of weeds—
What color is she now
When hidden behind dark clouds?

In spite of not being able
To see her white
Should I believe it is still white?

Instead of reducing her to familiar whiteness
Why not accept her mystery and freedom?
To assume colors
Unimaginable to me?
I do not know what color it is
Why not end up saying this?

That is why my mother
Shyaamaa of dark blue hue
Wears on her crown
The disk of the moon
Bent like an unyielding sickle
No beauty is just beautiful
My mother shows terrible beauty
Fascinating at the same time
In the shape of a sickle
Or the tongue dripping with blood

Another Dreamship

Another dreamship
Has reached the shore
Of my ageing and exhausted city
The welcome carpet,
Bright and golden,
Unrolls for me
And me alone,
Flanked on either side
By light-clad mantra deities
Ready with garland flowers
To sing:
Welcome, Shivaprakash
Your inheritors
From far off shores
Full of light and fragrance
Are waiting eagerly
For your advent
Do not look back
At the exhausted city
No need to carry anything from there,
Not even your poems
Embark soon
When the winds are favorable
The sky too is unusually clear
Unknown joys are tempting me
Unheard of melodies are calling
Unimagined fragrances are surrounding me

Goodbye! Exhausted city
For all you have given, not given
When I start walking towards
The golden ship
I hear the aggrieved voice
The nun, the protagonist of my play
'The Bride'
I wrote in my exile:
'Do not go
Till I reach my destination-
The Temple of Buddha of Compassion'
I have already retraced my steps
Goodbye! Golden ship
That voice is drawing me harder
Than all the promised joys
Of the far off land of my inheritors

Jesus On The Hill, Rio De Jenero

He is not like Atlas
Smarting under the weight
Of the globe

Neither is he like Alexander
That kingdom-grabber
Who wanted to eat up the earth
As if it was an apple

He stands erect and sleepless
On the crag on this night
Below him;
The earth, water and vegetation
The sleeping city
Lit up by a million lamps
Blinking like our mortal desires
At his back:
The indecipherable patterns
Of vagrant clouds
And hide and seek
Of twinkling stars

He has turned his back
To his homeland in heavens
And with his eyes closed

As if in contemplation
Spread his arms to the east and west
To forgive and embrace
All our cities of sin
And the nature which we
Have devastated
His compassion
Has no conditions

Stubborn Heart

Why does my heart, stubborn and stupid,
Go back to you again and again
Even after I said goodbye
Till next time?
Is it the tear hiding in the fear
In my aged heart
Of the inevitable end
Sudden and unexpected
Making all next times vanish?
Or is it the nostalgia
For the form that my youth
Sought take a palpable form
An audible voice
Long after youth
Bid me farewell in a shattered spring?
Or is it because
Of your touch that touched
That part of me
No touch could ever touch?
Or is it because of your pair of eyes
Which you hid long behind your specs
The eyes which were not eyes
But a pair of stars
Dark and diamond-like
On the firmament

Of my boundless heart's sky
Or in my bottomless desire's depth?
Or is it because
You are just you
Defeating similes and metaphors
Erect and established
In your uniqueness?
I can no more compare you
Who are so much you
To anything at all
That my mind creates
When enthralled by your magic

Why does my heart stubborn and stupid,
Go back to you again and again
Even after I said goodbye
Till next time?

Just a Little Longer

Just a little longer
Just a little longer
Lie down along with me
Just a little longer
Just a little longer
Dream on along with me
Just a little longer
Just a little longer
Breathe softly along with me

Just a little longer
Just a little longer
Your petal-like brows let me see

Just a little longer
Just a little longer
My Joy's closed bud you be

Just a little longer
Just a little longer
Let my eyes watch you like bee

Just a little longer
Just a little longer
Till you, a bud, flower I see

Just a little longer
Just a little longer
The day claims you from me

Just a little longer
Just a little longer
Till the moon unites you and me

Anywhere

This could happen anywhere
Because this is what is happening everywhere
It is not air but poison you breathe in
Anywhere
Countries are rich
GNP is rising everywhere
But people are starving
Dying or hurt fatally in accidents
Or cancer or boredom everywhere
While I wait here at a godforsaken airport
Or an abandoned railway station
For a flight or train to take me
To a country which issues no visas
While I wait I dream a dream
Within the dream within the dream
Of a garden in of love all dreamed
But no one dared to enter
Because happiness lives there in every tree
Even when they bear no flower or fruit
No one wants such fruits no one can eat
This can happen anywhere
They want to eat the fruit
Or flower when there is no fruit
Or leaves when there is no flowers
Or the tree when there are no leaves

No one can be happy anywhere
All are unhappy everywhere
For God is looking for the world She created
Which he actually never did
But which we did
Along with our unhappiness everywhere
Which can happen anywhere

Last Supper

Last supper over, Judas had betrayed Jesus again
For a few silver coins
In the garden of Gesthenene Jesus prayed
But God sent no angels
On the Cross Jesus cried Eli EliLammaSabkhtani
My Lord my Lord why have you forsaken me?
No answer came
But when he prayed
O Lord! Forgive them for they know not what they do
Then came Maria Magdalena
Who took Jesus
And they lived happily together
According to esoteric Bible
Bur people with faith
Know neither Jesus nor Maria Magdalena
They go round and round
In cycles of crime and punishment
Till they settle for religion of Satan
Where no forgiveness is possible
I pray to Jesus to open their eyes
So that they can see
That faith gets them nowhere
That only experience matters

For He resides in true hearts
Nowhere else
The Kingdom of God
Is only within

 Why am I drawn to this dark goddess
a dark moon amidst burning pyres
in the cremation ground
reflecting
the boring moon above
amidst burning stars..

This goddess, Shyama, putting out
her tongue dripping with blood
between protruding ivory tusks
also daubed with blood.

Her eyes flashing like lightning bolts
she laughs like thunder
breathes hurricanes
dances holding severed head
and sickle in hand

O who can resist her message has come for centuries
In my time world
But just the flash of eyelids in yours

I go on waiting
Till death
Beyond death
For my waiting for your message
Will outlive my million deaths

We Too Shall Pass

(A song for a fellow-poet)
The green in the grass
The red wine in the glass
Whisper to me always:
We too shall pass

The clouds in the sky
Its gold and silver eye
Whisper to me always
We too shall pass

The thrill of the first kiss
Love-making's bliss
Whisper to me always
We too shall pass

The rose and its sharp thorn
The woes of the love-lorn
Whisper to me always
We too shall pass

The great cities we built
And religion based on guilt
Whisper to me always
We too shall pass

The ocean's so boring
Only the river, inspiring
Speak in whispers always
We too shall pass

You and I too willgo
Our hills will be covered by snow
Despite beautiful rainbow
Our arrow's past won't go
They too whisper to us
You and we shall pass

Such passing is not a curse
How boring eternity's bliss
Let us worship the passing
Singing and dancing
Whispering again always:
This too shall pass

All is in a moment
Each poem, its monument
Which refuses to pass
When you and I will pass

In the garden of death
Let's write poems in mirth
Where nothing can survive
Our words will us revive
We know, all will pass
But poems will dare the impasse
Much longer than us

The World Theatre Day Poem

The World Theatre Day today
Has no theatre
The Theatre of the Heart today
Has its birthday
Actor one is on the shore of Bay of Bengal
The second, on that of the Pacific Ocean
The third, a woman actor, on the Alps
The rest of the dramatics personae
Are elsewhere
On the banks of other rivers and lakes,
The foot and peaks of other hills
Other houses in lanes and streets
Of other cities, towns and villages
In the play which I calling myself I
Am scripting all genres are mixed-
Tragedy, Comedy, Farce,
Opera, Kabuki, Prakarana
The more you move away
The closer it comes to you
Closer and closer
Future theatre when there is no future
Ona stage wider than void
All of us
He, she, you and I
Are playwrights, plays, directors

Producers, audiences, critics and theorists
Sometimes engaged in festive celebrations
Sometimes lamenting
Famine, deluge, holocaust
Or pandemics
No matter who dies
Who survives
There is no stage
But all is stage
No colours
But all colours
The stage with no restraints
Or constraints
The stage without stage
Theatre without theatre
The theatre of the heart
The theatre of the self
With no self

When Touch Is Tabooed

Let me touch you today
And also you, you and anyone
Without touching you
How sunlight touches the garden
Without touching it
How the stars touch each other
Without touching
How songs play in ears
Without touching them
How compassion touches the heart
Without touching it
We've touched too much between us
We have been too infected among ourselves
We enjoyed ourselves too much
No feelings
Getting sick among us
Every time we touch
getting too much joy
without giving it

Let us play today
Touch us
Without touching
Just giving
Without possessing
Just delivering

The distance is now deleted
Even if you are close
I'm far here on an ocean shore
You are far away on another coast
So far we can't touch each other with our hands
Only with our hearts
We can even see each other
Clearly from any distance
We can hear us
Without rushing to talk

Even our breathing
It's in tune
When the hearts touch
When souls touch each other

Until hands learn the lesson
They have forgotten for centuries
Until they remember why they started
To touch

Let them be hungry for touch
Until they learn again
To touch with the heart
To touch with the soul

How the guru touches the apprentice
In samadhi
How the ancestors touches us
In a vision
How the words of a dead poet
Touches the living

The Two Wings

The two wings of birds of light
In the land of the sun
Began to fight
The left wing said:
I am brighter than you
The right one said:
I am brighter then you
Tired of their non-stop flight
Said the bird of light:
Go down to the human realm
Transform into the two two eyes
Of an earthly nymph

Those two wings are your two eyes

Two petals of a lily
In the land of moon
Began to fight
Each saying:
'I am more beautiful'
The lily said go down to the human realm
And become eyelids of a princess

They became your two eyelids

I read this mystery
In your dark eyeballs
After I gave up deciding
Which of your eyes is brighter
Or which of your eyelids is more beautiful
I can perhaps never decide
I love them both
I kiss them both
When they open
It is my day
When they are shut
It is my night
Both of them are sweet to me

Says an Aboriginal Girl

After leaving my house
When I started
Missing my family
And living with new people
I can see the sun behind the glass
Lighting up a new beautiful day
Bringing me the aroma of coffee
Making me feel the pure mountain air
-Says, an aboriginal girl from Bibri community from Telamaca

Rain in San Jose

When rain started beating down
On a far off land defying all weather forecast
I was stranded in a building
About to close down
With the watchman
About to push me out into the merciless rain
You came in like kindness
To gift an umbrella
Thank you
It was no flood that evening
Nor was the umbrella Noah's ark
It was just what I needed at that moment
-a purely human need to weather
Unexpected rains in a far off land

Severed Head

Only after I suddenly saw your head
Severed from your body,
Shocked,
Did I notice your dead hands
Stained with so much blood of so many
Why this image?
Away from my sight
You, severed heads
You, blood-stained hands!
For even my imagination
Is becoming tainted with blood
Tell me O Aghora O Avalokiteshwara
Waters of which sacred ocean, river, pond
Can wash the blood from imagination?

Two Zeroes

Two zeros
Two truths

Zero One took an oath:
"I will be rid of all dirt and evil"
One by one it gave them up
"Get lost you lust
Get lost you hate
Get lost you six enemiesof the virtuous"
It went on chanting and,
Apart from the vices named above
It drove out other unnameable evils
Poor zero one's
It became half its huge size
And then said to itself:
"I will now get rid of the lesser good
And become even purer
If you compare one virtue to another, one is less the other is more"
After meticulous calculations, it lost all virtues
Thus zero 1 became just the zero
The symbol of nothing
Having watched this
Zero 2 learnt its lesson
And thought:

To consider anything completely evil
Is just a drivel
To the eye of compassion
Nothing is impure"
Saying thus it began to expand bringing into its
circumference of compassion
Everything
And became everything
Fondling everything with compassion
It transformed
The pomposity of virtue
The negativity of vice
With compassion, into compassion
And became the image of great compassion
Becoming the mother of all mothers of the earth
Becoming the voice of bodhisattva
And the symbol of
Not having anything high or low

O Guru Shivalinga
The 2 zeros are the two signs
You have given
Thank you!

Winter is My Season
(Agastyakutam, 30.1.2020)

Winter is my season
Not, like spring, all green
But yellow, mellow, slow,
melancholic and meditative
Some ageing leaves still struggle
To stay attached
To their home tree branch
Amidst leaves still enviably green
The other old ones
Say silent good byes
Stripped off the bygone green
To slide slowly down
Yellow, brown
Signing the air with the shapes
Of alphabets of my name
Some, stopped half way,
are held lovingly
By kind branches in loving twig fingers
Till a stronger wind blows them down
Some still want to keep delaying
The ultimate, inevitable descent
To the earth, the source, the mother
And fall so slow
They seem not falling

But trying to stop in between
Shaking
Shivering
The whole brittle being
So that every moment becomes
An eternity of leave's leave-taking
And travel down
Trembling in
Trepidation
Only a very few of them
Like hearts disenchanted
Dive straight down to earth
As if ever ready
For fall and the fall
The more playful ones
Let the lazy breeze
Divert them into streams
To journey along with the flow
Submitting to the flow
And becoming the flow
Fast or slow
Above
Below
Behold, my winter, my beloved
When the beautiful journey
Is from above to below
From pride to humility
From courage to surrender
Sooner or later
Onto earth or into water
My season is winter

The Conqueror

He first conquered the land
And its Inhabitants
We praised him
He next conquered the water
And its inhabitants
We praised him
He then conquered forests
And its birds, beasts and insects
We praised him
He then conquered the sky
With man-made metal birds
We praised him
Whatever he conquered
He went on subjugating
To the point of beating
Everything to pulp
We praised him
Raised monuments
Sang panegyrics
Because he had conquered us
Till he conquered air
That we breath
Which, in the triumphant
Hour of drunken blindness,
He poisoned

Making life-giving mother
An agent of murder
Murdering us
And also him
Who will praise him
After we die?
Who will praise him
After he dies?
But for now
Let us praise him
And his destructive exploits
Maybe for the last time
Till we last
Till he lasts

Seeking You

In the world that seeks
Hidden treasure
There is someone seeking
You beyond measure
Where every one with
Achievers teams
Someone secretly
Chases dreams
The world cries foul:
Wake up! You lazy
But there is some one
Who loves being crazy
More precious than
Gold and diamonds
To someone dew-drops
From unknown islands
Take the world away
From me you, wise
I am happy with my sky
Where secret moons rise

Silence

Silence! Neitzsches! Silence! Marx's!
God never died
Shut up atheists! God is still here
Everywhere
Was once upon a time
In the stone, plant, tree, insect,
Beast, bird
Later S/he assumed forms and shapes
In stone, metal, wood, gold and silver
God was never dead
S/he always existed
As form or formless
Human, animal, male, female or otherwise
As five elements, five suns,
Twelve moons, millions of stars,
Hurricanes, floods, wild fires
That devastated countries and the cities
Named after Her, Him or It
Becoming sometimes King or Queen
This or that Holy Book
Much later as Leader or Party
Her/is/It's latest incarnation is CEO
Or Advertizer Salesman, Banker
Tired of all forms anthropomorphic
Sick of all names in innumerable languages

He, She, It turned into currency
More important than breath
More important than food or drink
Currency that buys everything but nothing
That proliferates itself than any other thing
Living or non-living
The last God that demands the sacrifice
Of all earlier Gods
Regional, national and international
Religions and ideologies
Till all are equal in
Cashless bliss and total ananymity
Deaf God
Dumb God
Faceless, formless, nameless
Unfeeling**

My Beloved City

I will pass through you, my beloved city,
Only once
Like a ship with a merchandise of spices passing through a shore
Only once
Like a cloud shaped like a heavenly city
Passing through your sky only once
Like a mendicant with a moon-crown
Passing your door for alms
Only once
Like a snow flower appearing
In your sun-lit winter morning
Only once
Like a soft breeze that fondled your exhausted body unforgettably
Only once
I too will pass through you
Only once
O my beloved city
Of many joys
Of many taverns with oldest wines
Of temples with forgotten deities of the earth

I will bring nothing to you
I will take nothing from you

Only this fragrance I was born with
That comes with me everywhere
Will I will leave behind
For ever
Though I will pass though you
Only once
So that the fragrance will remind you of me for ever
Though I pass through you
Only once
Just as you pass through the time-world
Only once

Every night I pass through the same desert as you
Whether I am sleeping on the ocean shore
Or a hilltop or a valley or a plane
When all humans and animals are trudging along the same dreary landscape
Starved and thirsty for ages
None of us remember
Which paradise or kingdom
We lost or were expelled from
When every breath becomes an endless struggle
When only the stars
Our greatest ancestors are watching us
In silence and no compassion
We know they were there
Before we were here
And they will survive us and the desert
They give us no hope
But only a lesson in sad survival

O When will dawn
Return?

Kolkata
(3 AM April 26, 2014)

When I wake up from my broken sleep
This city, the lost love of my never-returning childhood,
the dream of my youth,
The stark reality of my disenchanted present
Is cuddled in deep sleep
Sleep so deep
That the unpredictable knives, country bombs
And revolvers
Do not figure, stab or explode in your dreams
Sleep my beloved lost dream of red oleanders
Perennial cloud-covered shravans
Eternal smiles as fleeting as lightening heart-stroke
I have lost you my precious dream
To the all conquering market
And all its glorious squalor

Why Not Leave Ageing Cities Alone

I love cities that resemble ageing loves
For there is something poignant and human
About growing old
And looking your real age

Those unpainted walls with fading paints
Smeared by the dust and smoke of the traffic;
Those rusted gates of what could have once been a garden;
Those balconies that hang out of many storied
Houses as ramshackle as almost abandoned visions;
Narrow lanes fighting their difficult ways through ghosts of crowded houses on either side;
Those sticky, greasy temples with layers of dried up oils where dwell silent deities once eloquent

Don't laughter at them
Don't insult them with repairs

Let them grow old in silence
Telling their stories in silence
Like an old courtesan whose beauty
Is now like the sad glory
Of a flame burning bright

Before something blows it out
In cruel kindness

How these leaves in autumn
Burn blood-red and golden yellow
Till winter comes

When the Poet Went to Sleep

She woke up in the dream world
Where stars were swimming
Like tiny fish in her river
She could turn the sun and the moon at will
Like a child can play with the wheels
Of a toy cart
Where she could cut, delete, correct or rewrite altogether her past
Like on her laptop
On screen of the sun
Reflected in her lake of the heart
The present stood like a loyal maid
Waiting eagerly for her slightest command
And future was calling her on the mobile
To ask in what costumes she could come for her audience
She heard sometimes in whispers
Sometime rolling like a thunder
All her forgotten lines
While lightning inscribed
On the horizon
Lines she would write a whole age later
She found at her feet
In her magic garden a tiny yellow flower
Its centre opened out
Into another constellation

With a hundred more suns
Surrounded by earths more glorious than ours
On one them she was pre-born
To see herself looking at this tiny flower
I watched all this happen in her dream
Like a still and silent hill
Watching the flow of seasons in the valley
Or formless space watching
The birth and death of mortal stars
And wrote it all down
On waking up
The poet had forgotten it all
When she saw this poem
I had calligraphed on her wall
Even then she remembered nothing
And thought it a wild fantasy
Of my making

One Moment

One moment, you said
Excellent, just one moment, I thought
But that one moment lasted longer than a whole life-
time, many life-times, centuries, millenniums and many
many time-cycles
As if you said: 'one moment'
in the lost city of Atlantis
buried somewhere now in ocean depths
like many cities destroyed
by fire, water or wars of men
As if I had heard you
in some distant utopian future
beyond cruelty of nature or men
beyond still unthought-of incurable contagions
we inflict upon ourselves
Ah, that one moment:
Civilizations rose and fell
Long-standing monuments
of human genius
too crumbled down
rivers rose in flood
volcanos spat out lace non-stop
earth quaked a million times
saints and prophets appeared
seeking cure ills of time

with timeless remedies
artists dreamt a million dreams
of the other sun, other moon, other stars
lighting undreamt-of worlds
You and I died
lived, died, unite and parted
times unnumbered
wearing and taking off
souls and bodies
times unnumbered
smelling flowers of perishable springs
braving the snows of repetitious winters

Your one moment
for you was just one moment
for me longer than eternity
neither time or timelessness
not a moment
not eternity

Take off Your Shoes

You there
off with your fancy shoes
The earth you tread on is scarred
Don't desecrate it with your
Spit
The earth you tread on is sacred
Walk gently
Don't stamp are stampede
The earth you walk on is sacred
Don't drill, bore, dig too often
Don't draw out all the underground water
The earth you walk on is sacred
Don't dirty it with your piss and shit everywhere
Recycle them into manure
to add to fertility
Don't uproot all trees
Aren't they your brothers and sisters
You Cain's progeny
The earth they stem from is sacred
Stop your trains, cars and trucks
Let the earth recover from all that strain
The earth you drive on is sacred
Rest your restless heart
Restless hands and legs
Driven by a delirious brain

Your body that came from the earth
And will return to the earth is sacred
For the earth you tread on is sacred
You infected every tree, plant
And even blades of grass
With your restless, scorching fever
Rest till it cools down
Rest till the the earth recovers
From the wounds you inflicted

Next time you walk
 walk gently
With reverence
Like through a sacred land

For the earth you tread on is sacred

The Tavern

So early at dawn today
O saki
The tavern is already full
There are more people
I saki
Than seats in your tavern
There are more lips
Thirsty and dying for wine
Than goblets at your tavern
How can you serve
So many
So much wine
With you two hands
Grow more hands saki
Get more wine casks

Look so many
Are queuing up at your door
There are more people
Waiting outside restlessly
So many
The queu is getting longer
And longer
As if the whole world
Is dying to enter your tavern to day

As many men as women
So many
Even if all the rivers turn into wine
Even if all the oceans are filled with wine
Even if clouds turn red
And rain wine winewine
There is not enough wine in your tavern
There is not enough wine in the world
Greater than all the rivers
Greater than all oceans
Is the thirst for wine today

You can't turn the thirsty away
You can't say no to them
But there are so many
So many
With just a pair of hands
With just a few goblets
with just a few casks of wine left
What will you do
What will you do
O saki?
Will you grow a thousand hands
Like Avalokteswara?
Will you multiply
Into millions?
Will the tavern grow into the world?
Or will the world turn into the tavern?
What miracle can make this happen
The saki?

When Thousands are Dying

When thousands are dying
because of pandemic or starvation
and we are reduced to watching them fall
unable to do much
other than offering tears and prayers
the morning comes again
after the night of my usual insomnia
with monotonous predictability
along with the same regularity-
the crows, sparrows and other birds
I can hear but cannot name

before the sun's rays enter my room
before the sun dawns somewhere in the east
it is another dawn in the corner
of my heart
your radiant face dawns like the sun in little
which unlike the sun
is never the same boring orb morning after morning
but looks different every day
more beautiful than ever before
Opening my the golden lotus
of my shriveling heart
Before the lakes of the earth
open their red lotus eyes

But when my eyes feast
on its ever changing beauty and glow
they are disappointed
as usual
because your face
is as pitiless to me
and as indifferent
as the sun
to the forest or desert
to the hill or valley
-the sun that burns itself out
to light up the whole world

Still
I wait for dawn in my heart
though the hope
seems to outlive me

I Told You

I told you, I told you
Not to follow her to her home
In the banana grove
In the impenetrable forest
On the ancient hill
But You wouldn't listen
If you had
If you had not followed her
If she had reached there alone
She would have turned into
An immortal banana plant
Amidst the mortal plants
Adding a new seatless species to life-forms
Every time she gave out
Pink flowers and red fruits
Her poems would
Burgeon and blossom
In new forms in our hearts
A million-fold

But you did not listen

You wanted her to stay human
Subject your reason and restraint
When you brought her back

To your palace
She could not recognise
You or your kingdom
The return had erased everything
From her mind and heart
Including her own name

She had already aged
Forgotten all her poems
About the green parrot
Bursting into passionate red songs
For all the trees to listen
She aged faster than you and me
And died a premature death

What a magnificent tomb
You built for her!

Exactly as I had foretold

The Moment's Hunt

'Look! Oceans of sorrow for a mustard of joy' -Allama

In the hair pore the size of a mustard
no joy even as tiny as a thousandth
of a mustard
When mustard turns into an ocean
in the cells of bones and muscles
mustards to mustards
O Shiva O Hara
pain painpain
vaster than the ocean
deeper than the ocean
No joy in the ocean
not even in the mustard
 Was it, is it there
in you?
Look look for it
in burning constellations
in you
Hunt O hunter
It is no joke
No moment's hunt
or eternity of pain
in you
in you Guru Shivalinga

The Black Flower

Of all the flowers
Our earth has given birth to
I love none of them
More
Than this pitch black flower
That flowers in the dense darkness
On enchanted new moon nights
Of hushed burial grounds
So dark
So small
And invisible to all
Except to my invisible eye
Which I borrow for a while
From fire-flies
Just for awhile
I too can't see it later

And I want none of you
To believe what I am saying
Maybe you too can see
This unseen flower
Only where it grows
Only when it flowers
If you borrow eyes
From from fire-flies

Three Mothers

Three mothers I saw
In three different dreams
I woke up from
More mothers I would have seen
Had I more dreams
Three mothers came and went
So fast
I that on waking up I
Know neither their names or looks
I asked three mothers in three dreams
Just one question:
Do you have O dream mothers somewhere
A mother outside these dreams
And how and where is she?'
The last one alone replied
Though not very clearly:
'Not just us but all things
Come from her
But the second part of your question
Has no answer, no meaning
It is difficult to fix her name or form
Because all comes from her
All names belong to her
And she lends them to beings
And takes them back

When she sucks them back again
Into her dark womb
Which is everywhere
Including this reply
And your poems
Which are all names given to her'

Last Night

You led me last night which was not the night
Not the day, not what is in between
But through some lands of oblivion
I would wake up at times with a mild pain
Every time I woke
You put me back to sleep and dream
Into a vortex of changing landscapes
You O mother leading me through
A dream exhibition of painful births
Killing either the mother or child or both
Through graves turning into cradles
Through revolutions that remake
And unmake the face of the earth
Through deluges that purge the earth
Of both the good and the bad paving the way
For the new
And then into the womb of earth and water
Where slept cites of buried magnificence
Like treasures in dreams
Like gold in ores
You showed me diamond crowns
And lofty towers
Covered with moss
Buried houses of slaves and artisans
Virgins worshipped and stabbed in sacrifice

To be kept in a huge pot like an artifice
Till I woke up to the chirping of birds
And to the dawn on an earth
Threatened with death
Still cursed and blessed
With the hope to survive
Sleeps, deaths and oblivions
O flower! O destruction!
O revolution! O annihilation!

O dark hand leading me through all
Landscapes invisible
To the clock and the calendar

Pain

I now know why my ribs and back
broke into pain
that has lasted sixty days and sixty nights
coming in and going
like my breath
now a tiny point
now a vast expanse
like my restless mind

Maybe because I was arrogant
and thought I could hold you
in my one big embrace

I thank no god
but only you
my ocean-girdled, cloud-crowned
Sun, moon and star-lit
earth-mother
O mother of all gods

I thank you for this pain
and the little morsels of day and night
you feed me
after making me
a globe-trotter into a prisoner

in my little rented home
which now
Is my bed, body
and the world

But for this blessing
I would perhaps
in the unbridled arrogance
of the world-conquering men
tried to hold you
in my greedy fist

which would have broken
my hands
and made me unfit
even to receive these precious morsels
of day and night
you kindly put into my hands

each morsel is sweet
for it keeps me from dying
but also bitter
for thousands are going

O mother
when were your morsels
only sweet or bitter
O bitter-sweet mother

O killer
O life-giver

Tiresias Warns

I see it all
you, Thebans, when you ask me
whose secret sin has brought this affliction
on the earth and water
on the living and non-living

born blind to your light
 I can see most clearly
what is hidden in the darkest of darknesses:

the secret sin
stems from all of you my fellow Thebans
the sin of killing your forebears
and violating your mothers

I your poet, prophet and ferryman
demand only Charon's wages—
a coin in each one of your mouths
already dead

Medea Matters

every morsel of meal
Medea is giving to her little boy and girl tonight
is heavenly
every grain is filled
with mother's boundless love
the more she feeds
the greater their appetite

but the bowl of mother's love
is no horn of course plenty
'Back to bed
back to bed dear ones'
whispers she
with an unusually quivering voice

sleep overpowers them soon
as they slip into sweet dreams of tomorrow

but only Medea knows
that the heavenly meal was poisoned
and that there will be no tomorrow

for her vengeance
must have its way...

vengeance against her treacherous man

tears in eyes
anger in the soul
she has already slit her children's throats

when innocence is murdered
both good and evil
will go up in conflagration

Like the sudden sunlight
In the dead of the winter
Painting snow-capped peaks golden

Like the unexpected soft breeze
Soothing the scorched body
On a desert in the worst summer

Like unforeseen showers
On a famine-stricken land

Like the dream of an enchanting goddess
On a boring sleepless night

You are swift, sudden and brief

But so difficult
To say goodbye to

Or forget even after many deaths
O dawn of a paradise
Lost forever

What City? What Light?

What city? What light?
What air? What smell?
What feel if wetness is this?
Of which river? Of which oceans?
What roads lead us there?
What other roads do they fork into?
What trees, what shadows are on your path?
What kind of wine in taverns there?
What flowers in gardens?
What palaces? What prisons?
Which is that bird fluttering free
Unmindful of chains and shackles?
What flowers in your hands?
What smile on your lips?
Who are you waiting for?
For the one groping towards you
To turn your silence into speech?

Do Not Wait Rajdip

Do not wait Rajdip
For Covid to end
To think of man, woman,
God or devil
To touch and feel
The end and the beginning
The birth, growth, death
And disappearance of a bird cry
The waves of breath and oceans
Falling and rising
Look closely
Every heart-beat and every pulse
Every closing and opening of eye lids
The stories of love, hate, jealousy, war and peace
Lasting a millennium
Played, replayed, paused and forwarded
In an hour or minuteor in the batting of an eyelid
Just the battling of an eyelid
Look the cosmos is happening
Look the cosmos is dead
All passing shadows of clouds
On hills, valleys, rivers and oceans
On deserts with shifting sands
Goodbye Egypt
Goodbye Rome

Goodbye Aztecs
Goodbye Mayans
Pyramids decay and grow
Temples built begin to flow
Sucked into and spewed out of
Black and white wholes
Here and now
All in here
Or nowhere at all
Open your senses
Make out of the stormy river of the mind
A mirror that reflects you
And then a break
And then a split
And then on explosion
In that moment or eternity
Look for that thing called I
Which is all and nothing
All and nothing are right here
In this moment
If you can, see, hear, taste
Touch and feel
Do not wait for something
To end
Because all ends are beginnings
Sometimes old
Sometimes new

The Poet's Silence

The poet's silence-
like Shiva in meditation-
a sharp arrow that lodged the heart ages ago
the sweet notes of beluva-bird amidst the mist of dawn
the life breath struggling to creep back into the body declared dead
a brilliant constellation
dimmed among storm clouds on a dark night
the ephemeral station for the rod of sunlight entering the closed room through the small window
the pause of cascading waters in the slowed stream of the valley
the mysterious dream wriggling out of the dark cave of sleep
the shame of aggressive intellect proclaiming its own omniscience in its sleepless wakefulness
the unending narration of pasts and futures in the transient languages of ever changing present
the multitudes of wild aghories celebrating the day on the darkest new moon night in the cremation ground
the fraction of the fraction of a second of the ultimate joy of sweet union somewhere in the midst of centuries and millenniums
a basil garden where the sun never sets and the stars never dim
in the reimagined memory of an ordinary day when one tasted the immortal drink
all, in this moment
the monument
of the evanescent

AnAnti-Poem

(Courtesy the Marathi poet VindaKarindikar)
"When he was a boy
he urinated in the Arabian sea
and spent the rest of his lifetime in measuring the rise
in the level of the sea water"
This other one when young
defecated near the Himalayas
and then ordered the wise of the earth
to measure and report to him
the increase in the height and the breadth of the
mountain ranges from Pamir Plateau to Myanmar
This command he whispered in such sweet whispers
melodiously, smoothly, in the half silence of his measured
half language
that the wise of the earth from different disciplines
different temperaments
set out immediately
to produce new instruments of measurement to measure
the ever increasing height and breadth of the mountain
after his historic defecation
The wiser still are trying to understand
the cryptic message
of his command so difficult to understand
by transporting and translating his words
into many lands, language and epochs
engaging in the ultimately failed attempt
to understand his message in order to make others
understand
Astrologers are trying by creating new almanacs
to understand the exact planetary significance

of his defecation
whereas
sociologists and fateologists are busy investigating the
ways and life styles that caused him to defecate just when
and just where he did it
Most important of all
silenceologists are trying to address
the metaphysical causes
why he has not been creating
Anything after defecating
-a problem highly suffocating

To Monsinor Romero

Because most live only for themselves
Just a few live for others
Fewer still die for others
We who are not so mean as to live only for ourselves
We who have no courage to die for others
Let us learn to live
For what those few die for
15-6-2017, San Salvador

A Sudden Glance

A sudden glance, an unexpected scent-
That is what sealed our unending bond
O myeternity made of fleeting moments

The Desert

Every night I pass through the same desert as you
Whether I am sleeping on the ocean shore
Or a hilltop or a valley or a plane
When all humans and animals are trudging along the same dreary landscape
Starved and thirsty for ages
None of us remember
Which paradise or kingdom
We lost or were expelled from
When every breath becomes an endless struggle
When only the stars
Our greatest ancestors are watching us
In silence and no compassion
We know they were there
Before we were here
And they will survive us and the desert
They give us no hope
But only a lesson in sad survival
O When will dawn
Return?
When the priest returned late at night
To offer nocturnal worship to the goddess
His hands were full of dirt and sweat
She stood on the steps of marble mantap
Sweet talking to her companion- the moon

Tiny Blue Flower

In the light of morning sun, I saw a tiny
Blue flower risen from earth. Sudden clouds!
Let us mourn and celebrate evanescence

Exile

No more will I long
For a single flower
In your garden
Where a thousand flowers
Bloom to wither
No more will I long
For a single home
In your city
Where a thousand have homes
Rendering thousands more homeless
No more will I seek
A place to sit, stand or sleep
In your your grand palaces
Trembling in trepidation
Of its own undeserved splendour
No more do I want to be a moment
In your succession of moments
Where each new moment devours the old
While being devoured by the next moment
Count me out of your places and times
As I, born prematurely after death,
Am displaced beyond restoration
In your refugee camps
And condemned to a rock garden
Exiled from springs and winters
Between volcanoes and earthquakes
Neither changing nor repeating

Your Name

On the firmament
I found a star
Brighter to my eyes
Than all others
I called it by your name
In a garden
I entered in my dream
I saw a flower
Lovelier to my eyes
More fragrant
To my nostrils
Than all the others
I called it by your name
In a erasure-trove
I sighted in a dream
I found a diamond
Brighter than others
To my eyes
Dearer to my heart
Than all the others
I called it by your name
All this happened
In dreams I dreamt
Before I dreamt you, me
Or the world

--the reason why
Your name is sweeter to my tongue
Dearer to my soul
Than you, me
Or the world

The Lotus

I waited long for the fog to clear
So I could see that lotus
Said to bloom only on this lake
But when at last when the fog cleared
It is your face, not the lotus, that appeared
I waited all through the night
For the dawn to break
And the sun to rise dispelling the darkness
But when the sun rose at last
It is your face, not the sun,
That shone on the eastern horizon
I waited the whole evening
For clouds to clear
So that I could see that star
That adorned the moon
But when the cloud at last cleared
I saw, not the star with the moon,
But the star with your face
I see your face overlooking me
Since then
All day, all night,
In dreams and wakefulness....
Yes, your incomparable face
As beautiful and as tortured
As the piece of earth

I grew up on
Which is also my country
And the world
When I lay half-awake this morning
My bed became a stretcher
When I was half-awake
An angle whose face was not visible
As I was half-awake
Was pushing the stretcher I lay on
When I was half-awake
Over sun- lit clouds,
Among stars of the vast sky
Through dawns and dusks in the valley
Through battle fields full of screams
Through sacred places resounding with mantras
Which I half heard
As I was half-awake
When I smelt an unworldly fragrance
We were approaching
When I was half awake...
When I was fully awake
I was back on my bed
Which was no more a stretcher
The angel too had vanished
Into the morning lights
Along with all landscapes
Seen, heard, felt, smelt
when half awake
I was now fully awake..

Like A Pearl

Like a pearl in the ocean's depth
Like a fountain among rocky mountains
Like layers of gold in the rawness of the ore
Like the star in the sky of an ordinary day
Like the healer among the mortally sick
Like a princess in the sorcerer's dungeon
You too are hidden
From all mortal eyes
Even from your own
But my third eye
Has found you, O precious one
If you don't believe
See for yourself
In the magic mirror
I have made only for you

Crocodile

When crocodile sheds tears
Stones grows on fields
Pythons become frogs' protectors
Jackals found churches
The stars go blind to each other
Lifeless things lead by hand
Humans turned into metals
The sun and the moon are not sure
Whether to set or rise
Poems can only rage and ran

Do Not Thank

Do not thank O orange orchard
The fruit gatherer
What could he gather without you?
Do not praise O clouds
The drenched earth
It would be all parched
Without you?
Do not praise O sun
The tiny disk of the sun
What light could it reflect
Without you?
Do not praise O flower
The honey bee
What honey could it gather
Without you?
Do not praise O breath of speech
The idle poet
What poem could he make
Without you?

The Priest

The priest went to the lotus pond
To wash his dirty hands
But when he turned to the goddess
He saw that the water that washed his hands
Had washed away the whole scene-
The mantap, the steps, the goddess and the moon

On Your Face

On your face I have seen the light
That shone before the first dawn
On your lips I have seen a smile
That smiled before humans learnt to smile
In your voice I have heard a song purer
Than songs of the first birdsong
In your breath I have felt a fragrance
Of the age before all our forests
I waved you goodbye on a dream platform
When a crowded train pulled in
Without even shaking hands you got in
The train moved on along with the dream
I woke up on the earth that quaked last night
And wrote for you this trembling poem

Tell me in the next dream how I should
Send it to you from the world I woke up to

Farewell
(To Shukracharya Rabha)

When we cremated your mortal body
In the midst of sal trees
That housed a mind
That deserved immortal fame
We could not hear
The whisper of salt trees
Waving in the wind:
'How vain!
Immortality has no name
No fame
Look at us
We continue to be immortal
Without fame'
No wonder you named
your theatre
Under the Sal Tree

Two Green Spirits

Warned my story-telling grandmother:
'Because you were born in an inland city,
beware of two green spirits that will challenge you
when you go to a seashore city-
The roaring spirit of the sea
And the silent spirit in women's eyes'
How could I ignore the warning
Of a wise old women born
In the ocean of stories?
So I chose, when challenged,
Not to respond
And began to gather sands and shells
And pluck and smell a red butterfly flower
From a small garden someone had grown
On the shore

Tangiers, Moracco

Somewhere in this huge city
Surrounded by the bluish green sea
Entering the greenish blue ocean near a light house
?Washed by constantly restless waves
Somewhere in this huge city
Whose roads always surprise
With sudden falls and rises
Somewhere in this city
Where millions come and go
To watch its magic and splendour
Somewhere in this city
Where millions struggle
To make a home
Somewhere in the city
Where the sun shines brightest
Competing with the equally bright moon
And where night lamps below
Challenge the wakeful stars above
Somewhere in this city
I lost my keys
That could open
What could have been
My impermanent home
In a life before my lives
Return it to me

O sun O moon O stars O street lamps
Return it to me
Even if you find it in a life
After all my lives
Let me find the key
That opens the door
Of my one and only impermanent home
In this city of sweetest oranges
Whose harbour has seen
Ships and merchandise
From all lands of men
Century after century

While in Chalkidiki, Greece

Drive with no destination in mind
Tear up your map
Switch off your navigator
Just drive following the roads
Winding round and round
Green hills and valleys
Golden shores of the sapphire sea
Have no plans or expectations
If you do as I have told you
Every minute is a discovery
Unthought of
undreamt of

The Rainbow

Look!'I said to him.'Look! A rainbow all over your chest!' He did not hear me. Or pretended not to. As I had never seen before a rainbow-clad human body , I started shouting louder and louder, 'Look...' At last some people heard me but thought it a joke. When he too heard he could neither see nor believe.
I have stopped telling people they are becoming rainbows.
And he has since written a scientific book on why humans and rainbows cannot become each other.
It has become a compulsory textbook in S chills universities.
There are so few who see or spot sudden rainbows these days

Why Write Poetry?

Why write poetry?
Go ask the wind
-why do you blow?
Go ask the fire
-Why do you burn?
Find out and tell me
Why clouds float
Why woods turn green
Why ice melts down
Why stones crack up
Why shyness causes blush
Why the sun and the moon
Rise and set, set and rise
Why the rain- bearing cloud
Carries thunder and lightning bolts
Find out, find out
And let me know
Even after you gather
and let me know all answers,
I cannot tell you, Mr critic,
Why I write poetry

Playthings

Some playthings we made
With our own mischievous hands playfully
In our childhood-
We named them
As they could not name themselves:
God, goddess, king, queen, commander and priest
How comes it now
That we have forgotten that?
We think and believe
In our grown- up present
That they can make or unmake us,
Their makers
Is this what is meant
By growing up
In our schools and societies?

www.ingramcontent.com/pod-product-compliance
Lightning Source LLC
Chambersburg PA
CBHW031120080526
44587CB00011B/1052